GEC

PRIES

KENNETH MASON

SLG PRESS
Convent of the Incarnation
Fairacres   Oxford
0X4 1TB

© THE SISTERS OF THE LOVE OF GOD 1980

ISBN 0 7283 0083 4
ISSN 0307-1405

ACKNOWLEDGEMENT

*The picture of George Herbert on the cover is from the
drawing by Robert White and is reproduced by kind permission
of the Houghton Library, Harvard University*

I

'THE COLLAR'

GEORGE HERBERT was born in April 1593 and died of consumption in 1633, just short of his fortieth birthday and only three years after being ordained priest.

Herbert discovered the meaning of faith as most of us discover it, through sin and repentance, suffering and patience, the agony of decision and the serenity of hope. But unlike most of us he was a saint. And in his journey to sanctity Herbert's gift of poetic inspiration took up and transformed his common Christian experience, making it articulate in his verse. It is, indeed, through his poetry that Herbert continues to minister to us.

So for us his priesthood is in his poetry. He does not speak of things we have not encountered, he has no doctrine of his own, but through his poetry he purifies our knowledge of the things which as Christians we already know. Poetry is not merely a way of writing, it is a way of perceiving. The poet's distinctive way with words allows him to say what without it he could not say, but also forces him to see more clearly, feel more sharply, what otherwise he would feel and see only in a confused manner. The price of this may be great. The confused state of our perceptions protects us from painful knowledge and, to renounce confusion, while it may allow a certain devastating beauty to emerge, is first of all an act of decision not to avoid that pain. This was Herbert's decision—a man for whom, as his verse shows, real decision was always bitter. But through it he became not only a poet of rare power but also a teacher of the Church, a guide along that way in which experience is transformed by faith.

* * * * * *

I struck the board, and cry'd, No more.
                    I will abroad.
          What? shall I ever sigh and pine?
My lines and life are free; free as the rode,
          Loose as the winde, as large as store.
                    Shall I be still in suit?
          Have I no harvest but a thorn
          To let me bloud, and not restore
          What I have lost with cordiall fruit?
                    Sure there was wine
Before my sighs did drie it: there was corn
                    Before my tears did drown it.
          Is the yeare onely lost to me?
                    Have I no bayes to crown it?
No flowers, no garlands gay? all blasted?
                    All wasted?
          Not so, my heart: but there is fruit,
                    And thou hast hands.
          Recover all thy sigh-blown age
On double pleasures: leave thy cold dispute
Of what is fit and not. Forsake thy cage,
                    Thy rope of sands,
Which pettie thoughts have made, and made to thee
          Good cable, to enforce and draw,
                    And be thy law,
While thou didst wink and wouldst not see.
                    Away; take heed:
                    I will abroad.
Call in thy death's head there: tie up thy fears.
          He that forbears
          To suit and serve his need,
          Deserves his load.
But as I rav'd and grew more fierce and wilde
          At every word,
Me thoughts I heard one calling, *Child!*
          And I reply'd, *My Lord.*

'THE COLLAR'

This poem, 'The Collar', is superficially unusual among Herbert's works, in the coarseness of much of its expression and the irregularity of its metre and rhyme. Only superficially however, for his intrinsic delicacy and control have not been abandoned. It is his fine sense for words which chooses the rough expression here and his technical mastery which makes this free metre serve his purpose. Disorder and violence are allowed to be themselves and yet are contained. At bottom the principle is ascetical. God's way with man is such that it excludes nothing and finally transforms everything. Just as a confession must be true and full to be a confession at all, or as a sacrifice offered in thanksgiving must be wholly burnt upon the altar, so man can reserve no experience to himself and keep it back from God. Even the desire to exclude God, the feeling of resentment against him, the mood of rebellion, can and must be brought to him.

Freedom and vitality go together. Human relationships tend to suppress both for safety's sake. We recognise it as a good friendship or a good marriage when emotions are not suppressed and people respect one another enough to be themselves in each other's company. How much more so when the friend is God! Herbert's way with God is conversational, direct and vital, and if this gives him freedom to say frankly that he loves God, it also gives him freedom to say that he hates him. There is no mere artifice in the antagonisms of this poem. He is not just testing how far he can go, still less feeling his way into a rebelliousness that is not his own. He means what he says. He has been confined and now he will call it confinement. He is weary of the Christian way, its perpetual restraints and its lack of rewards.

No fewer than five of Herbert's poems are called 'Affliction'. It was, for him, a characteristic of all experience. Seldom in good health from boyhood, depressive and procrastinating in temperament, forced to manage the unhappy moods he could not escape, torn between ambitions, he achieved his destiny to be a priest only late in his short life of less than forty years. All the while, though, he wrote his poetry. As he himself put it, it was the record of 'the many spiritual conflicts' betwixt God and his soul 'before he could subject his own will to the will of Jesus', his Master.

Conflict and contradiction—that was how he saw it himself. From

3

early days he was intended for the priesthood—by his own will, it seems, as much as that of his eminently impressive mother. Yet other possibilities attracted him as well, and genuine humility held him back. At the university his desire to learn divinity had somehow to coexist with a talent for rhetoric, and it was the latter rather than the former that won him his appointment as Public Orator, a position on the borderland between scholarship and the life of the Court. The King held out promise of advancement in his service—no trivial promise to a man of noble family. The attractiveness to him of other things could only mean that his heart was not wholly for the priesthood and, if not, then how could he be a priest? And if that were not enough, sickness also inhibited action and delayed decision. One can argue for ever about what finally gets a man to make up his mind, but Izaak Walton was probably right in thinking that the death of King James had much to do with it, as well as the encouragement of his family and William Laud's persuasion. It was not so much that he had to calculate his worldly prospects afresh as that a bond which had tied him emotionally to the world was broken.

Herbert is noted for the use of ambiguity in his verse. Looking at his life, we may feel this is no more than a reflection of his character. Yet ambiguity was itself a master 'conceit' of poetry in his time. It is the culture to which he belongs, the predicament of his age, which speaks through him in this. In so far as his age was like our own he speaks for us as well. If you are committed to doing the will of God, as Herbert and the society to which he belonged were committed, though that will can only be grasped through faith, a faith which cannot be taken for granted, then your position is ambiguous. Those who are gifted with inner liberty will feel this most keenly.

In a delightfully ironical poem called 'Decay', Herbert looks back to the Old Testament period when God was sensibly present in history and society, plain to be grasped:

> One might have sought and found thee presently
> At some fair oak, or bush, or cave, or well.

With pagan nostalgia he regards that period as a golden age from which the present is a decline. God has moved from the public to the private

4

sphere. We have to search within ourselves to find him, and do battle there against disproportionate odds to acknowledge him.

> But now thou dost thyself immure and close
> In some one corner of a feeble heart.

In spite of the New Covenant, in spite of the grace of Christ, Herbert can say, 'I see the world grows old'! People in our own time have spoken about the 'privatisation of religion' and 'the sense of the absence of God' and have inquired into the consequences for faith of these things, but Herbert shows us that there is nothing particularly new in this. He too knew what it was to serve God in a world from which God was apparently absent, and with a heart that was only half disposed by nature to a Christian interpretation of life.

In 'The Collar' he expressed the torment of that knowledge. This poem is more than a protest against suffering, or the record of a sudden decision to give way to temptation. It is the cry of a man torn apart by the ambiguity of Christian existence. The 'collar' is a metaphor for discipline. We often distinguish sharply between self-discipline and imposed discipline, failing to see that all discipline depends both upon our own will and the supportive will of others. A man is given freedom to revolt against the discipline he has himself embraced whenever he perceives afresh the part of the others against his own. A small shift of perspective and he can attribute the narrowness of the path he has followed to their hostility. So here, Herbert, who had called God his Lord, and as we shall see will call him Lord again, is momentarily disposed to call him his tyrant. The energy he has expended, the satisfactions he has renounced, in order to serve God appear now, in this moment, to be a waste. He has missed an opportunity to serve himself far better than God has served him.

> Is the yeare onely lost to me?
> Have I no bayes to crown it?
> No flowers, no garlands gay? all blasted?
> All wasted?

From this, the explosive mid-point of the poem, its mood becomes like Herbert's own, 'more fierce and wilde', bolder in its antagonism

toward God and yet more desperate. The confidence that anger has in-
spired is short-lived. The louder it shouts the more breathless it appears.
Rebellion is already falling apart in disorder when God calls, 'Child!',
rebuking Herbert and yet recalling him to a peace which his self-
assertiveness had abandoned.

Herbert, we have seen, speaks as a man of his time and so, perhaps,
the more effectively to our time since we have here 'two worlds become
much like each other'. He serves God as we do in a world in which the
service of gain or pleasure or the honour of men has more plausibility
than God's service, in which therefore the service of God is never under-
taken for long without a sense of contradiction. Being a Christian, being
a priest, does not make God's rivals less attractive or his command-
ments less of a constraint or his call to self-denial less of a crucifixion.
In the first flush of conversion or ordination we may think that it does,
and even testify to others that it does. We sense that the presence of
God is an indefectible determinant of our lives. Nor are we deluded in
this, for it is God's way with beginners, to let them walk by sight until
they have been prepared for the darkness of faith. But in the way of
faith this protection is withdrawn. We become aware that satisfactions
far more palpable than any God has so far given are slipping by. Torn
between hope and regret we may feel moved to protest against the
God whose love constrains us, and our resentment against him is hard
to keep in.

Herbert's testimony throughout this poem is that we need not keep
it in. The poetry of the Gospel is able to contain our rebellion just as
Herbert's verse contains even the sentiments of 'The Collar' without loss
of integrity. We need not be afraid to admit the fleeting or deep-seated
resentments that develop within us. God himself is best fitted to cope
with the grievances that arise against him. When we are angry at the
way he has disposed our lives, we *may* be angry, since he can take it.
When we have a grudge against the narrowness of our narrow way we
need not bottle it up where it will only work secretly to destroy us; we
can let it out and challenge God to justify his ways. God alone can
meet that challenge. If we try to protect God and meet it ourselves the
most favourable result can be only a pathetic illusion—a gospel rooted
in the dexterity of men and not in the faithfulness of God, uncertain of

of its own ground, mistrustful of the grace to which it testifies, degenerating into bigotry.

Herbert's example here looks forward to modern psychology, but it also looks back to the origins of the Christian tradition. The psalmists too complain at the absence of God, the obscurity of his ways, the vanity of serving him. They feel free to complain.

> We have heard with our ears, O God, our fathers have told us: what thou hast done in their time of old . . . But now thou art far off.

> Lo, these are the ungodly, these prosper in the world, and these have riches in possession: and I said, Then have I cleansed my heart in vain, and washed mine hands in innocency.

And Jesus himself, in the prayer of Gethsemane and the cry of dereliction on the cross, shows at once a far deeper bitterness and a still wider freedom.

II

'LOVE'

Love bade me welcome: yet my soul drew back,
      Guiltie of dust and sinne.
But quick-ey'd Love, observing me grow slack
      From my first entrance in,
Drew nearer to me, sweetly questioning,
      If I lack'd any thing.

A guest, I answer'd, worthy to be here:
      Love said, You shall be he.
I the unkinde, ungratefull? Ah my deare,
      I cannot look on thee.
Love took my hand, and smiling did reply,
      Who made the eyes but I?

Truth Lord, but I have marr'd them: let my shame
      Go where it doth deserve.
And know you not, sayes Love, who bore the blame?
      My deare, then I will serve.
You must sit down, sayes Love, and taste my meat:
      So I did sit and eat.

This poem stands last in *The Temple*, like a summary of all that
Herbert had experienced at God's hands, and all that he had to teach.
For that reason we must not suppose that it refers only to one in-
cident, or to one kind of experience. Not this particular mercy, or that
Christian ordinance, but the whole of life is Love's feast, and every act
of grace re-asserts God's invitation to share in it. Nevertheless, it is not
wrong to find a reference to Holy Communion in this poem. In the
New Testament, the symbolic power of the Eucharist includes the more
general meaning of the meal, the feast and the banquet, as well as its

specific link with the death of Christ. And in Herbert's own work we see what value the Sacrament had for him, not simply as an element in Christian worship but as central to his awareness of God's love. It is not in a poem on the Eucharist but on Gethsemane that he writes,

> Love is that liquor sweet and most divine,
> Which my God feels as bloud; but I, as wine.
>
> ('The Agonie')

That is not the language of devotion, if by devotion we mean something distinct from the exercise of faith as such, reserved to a particular occasion or a particular mood. Herbert does employ a 'devotional' language; there are things he says on approaching the Sacrament which are tied to the sacramental moment, but he knows also that such language can miss the depth of intimacy and breadth of reference which a full apprehension of the Sacrament conveys. There is something incongruous about the liturgical communication of God's grace, the ritual embodiment of his loving-kindness. For while the love may stir up a like love in us, the ritual context qualifies and may inhibit the freedom which that love should inspire. Liturgy emphasises the authority and dignity of the one to whom it is addressed. It seeks to recognise God's divinity, but in so doing it divinises him according to man's understanding of divinity. The sense of awe and terror may be communicated far more immediately than the astonishing sense of grace. Herbert tells us that this aspect of the Eucharist certainly dissuaded him from offering himself for the priesthood.

> O what pure things, most pure must those things be,
> Which bring my God to me!
>
> ('The Priesthood')

And after ordination his terror of the sacramental occasion is not diminished:

> The Countrey Parson being to administer the Sacraments, is at a stand with himself, how or what behaviour to assume for so holy things. Especially at Communion times he is in a great confusion, as being not only to receive God, but to break, and to administer him.
>
> (*The Country Parson*)

Now if the poem 'Love bade me welcome' speaks in a different tone
from that, we are not to see this either as evidence of repentance or as
regrettable inconsistency. The incongruousness of God's love for man,
whether enshrined in the liturgy or discovered in simple domestic circumstances, is not to be overcome by anything we can do. It will
always, in some way, surpass our ability to grasp it. Reverence, for
Herbert, was not something to be repented of, but his concern in this
poem is for the way in which the God who inspires reverence, nevertheless, in spite of reverence, takes possession of our hearts.

Herbert shows himself, at the beginning, uncertain, diffident and ill
at ease in his approach. He gains confidence through the look and smile
and touch of love. It is not an overwhelming experience—rather very
gentle and peaceable—yet we sense that a great obstacle to enjoyment
has been removed, that a quite fundamental truth has been grasped.

The poem can well be compared with Cranmer's Prayer of Humble
Access. Like Cranmer, Herbert is saying, 'We do not presume to come
to this thy table trusting in our own righteousness'. It is not, of course,
surprising to find an echo of that prayer in the work of an Anglican
priest deeply attached to the Prayer Book; and yet there is a difference.
Cranmer gives us the well-sifted Christian words to say, and we say
them. He finds the right sentiments, born of the right doctrine, and
places them upon our lips. Such a proceeding is natural in a liturgist,
especially if, like Cranmer, he is convinced that even the subjective con-
tent of worship can be stated in the liturgy. Herbert however, in this
poem, implicitly denies the truth of that approach. Access to God is
never so straightforward. Ideas and sentiments that the liturgy cannot
include nevertheless demand recognition and may get seriously in the
way. Herbert draws these ideas and sentiments into his poem; he plays
with the licensed alternatives to direct humble access—we can even say,
he teases. There is a playful perversity in the way he shows himself
resisting love before, in the end, he surrenders to it.

Herbert has the reputation of a humble man, and this is a poem of
humble access, but what is humility? Here we have humility in its complexity, even its antagonism against itself. There are two humilities, not
one. One is the achievement of God's grace and a fitting response to it.
The other is so compounded of the feelings of shame, unworthiness and

irretrievable debt that it resists the grace of God, even while recognising it as grace. For the most part this poem is about the second. The first is achieved only in the final words, in an act of truth and obedience. But, to begin at the beginning.

> Love bade me welcome: yet my soul drew back,

He feels guilty and unworthy, and the only proper action upon the knowledge of these things is to go away. The invitation is sincere and well-meant. Love meets his hesitation with 'sweet' enquiry—that is, clean and without aspersion. Nevertheless the host does not really know whom he has invited. A guest who is really worthy must be found.

> Love said, You shall be he.

Those whom Love invites are worthy by virtue of the love that invites them. But Herbert, and all who share his hesitation because they cannot find this worthiness in themselves, hold back in embarrassment. If the host knows his own mind, still he takes no account of his guest's feelings.

> . . . Ah my deare,
> I cannot look on thee.

and again,

> . . . let my shame
> Go where it doth deserve.

Shame and embarassment may seem better than pride and self-confidence, yet their effect is still to prevent any true participation in God's love. 'Better' on a scale of human values, they still represent a kind of human assertiveness, and are no more open to grace than the qualities we think of as their opposites. Divine love changes the entire basis of the relationship between man and God. Now it must show that the basis is changed. Herbert has confessed his feelings and thinks they are a sufficient reason for his withdrawal. Love's next answer denies that. It is not feeling that must count but the objective fact, the work that Love itself has performed.

> And know you not, sayes Love, who bore the blame?

Of course, like us all, he knows and does not know. He believes and doubts. Faced with the unanswerable answer to our doubts we do not give in, we wriggle. Herbert's poetic skill and spiritual sensitivity triumph beautifully at this point as he shows us man, still squirming, still determined to have his own way, even though a way marked by the most profound humility. In this position the Prodigal said, 'I am no more worthy to be called your son. Make me one of your hired servants'; Peter protested, 'Lord, you shall never wash my feet', implying, 'but I will wash yours'. And Herbert says directly,

> My deare, then I will serve.

Somewhere within us there is a suspicion that the grace of God cannot be, cannot be *allowed* to be, total, entire grace. Perhaps it is disbelief, perhaps it is resentment that God's mercy should be absolute and leave us neither need nor ground to contribute to our own acceptance. We are aware that God has given his all for us, but we want somehow to make it up to him, to give him back the equivalent of what he has given us. So we accept his forgiveness not as an absolute discharge but as a form of probation. We recognise his generosity and then chastise ourselves for our lack of gratitude, as though gratitude itself has to pay back all that generosity had originally given.

Herbert once changed the title of a poem from 'The Second Thanksgiving' to 'The Reprisall', pointing up, by just this shift of emphasis, the intimate link betweeen giving back and getting one's own back. Like 'Love' it is a poem about man's unwillingness to surrender entirely to grace.

> I have consider'd it and finde
> There is no dealing with thy mighty passion:
> For though I die for thee, I am behinde;
> My sinnes deserve the condemnation.

There is no *dealing*, no *trading*, with the love of the crucified Christ. We want to pay him for his gift of himself, our death for his death, our free service for his free love. But however much we may approximate to such an exchange—for indeed, as Herbert says, we may die for him—we never achieve a true equality.

'I have consider'd it,' is no mere rhetorical preamble in this poem. Herbert is admitting that he had indeed considered 'dealing', that is, had intended trading with Christ in the matter of his passion. He has found the intention frustrated, and only now considers that commerce with such love is impossible. Grace is always grace. If we die for Christ it is in the power of his death; if we serve him freely the freedom is his gift; if we confess our sins in grief it is by his truth at work in us. Beyond this we cannot and must not try to go. Christ did not die for sinners to make them worse sinners—to make the desire for self-justification more desperate.

Love bids us welcome. God, who has made us without our aid and intends to reward us beyond all our deserving, bids us welcome. And when our sad humility protests that he cannot go so far and we will not be honoured in this fashion, then he deals firmly with us. Quick-eyed Love, observing, anticipating, taking us by the hand, smiling tenderly and ironically, tells us not to be silly.

> You must sit down, sayes Love, and taste my meat:
> So I did sit and eat.

III

'AARON'

THERE have been priests who were poets and poets who happened to be priests but seldom have the two vocations been combined so effectively in union with one another as in George Herbert. Indeed, with him it is hard to speak of two vocations. There is a single calling, acknowledged, received and fulfilled within a single life, and at every stage the man who lived this life engaged with it through the medium of poetry. If then we should ask, where does Herbert express most fully his convictions about the Christian priesthood, the answer can only be, in his verse. Certainly there is also his prose work, *The Country Parson*, but that, precisely because it was written 'as a mark to aim at', stands at some distance from his most intimate thoughts. Even though we can recognise the same convictions in both prose and verse the prose speaks in public about generalities, and is not without a strain of moralism, while the verse is always conceived in the liberty of the present moment in conversation between himself and God. Herbert's thought on the matter of priesthood then, is to be found diffused throughout the body of his verse, and especially concentrated in the two particular poems which treat of the subject, 'The Priesthood' and 'Aaron'.

'The Priesthood' is the statement of a man who is so engaged by the idea of priesthood that, if it be God's will, he cannot fail to become a priest, and yet who at this stage is offering his reason for not doing so. There is only one reason, that he is not worthy of so holy a task. If priesthood were simply a state to be aspired to, Herbert could tell himself that he enjoyed a higher status in the eyes of men already. If it were simply a task to be fulfilled, he would have to acknowledge that he had the ability to fulfil it. Such questions, which weigh heavily in the case of some aspirants to ordination, are neither here nor there in Herbert's case. There is only one obstacle, as we have seen in looking at 'Love', that he lacks the holiness worthy of such a holy calling. And since worthiness is not to be acquired but can only be received by

14

submission to the love which bestows worthiness, Herbert's refusal lacks conviction even as he states it. It is not a matter of what to do, but when.

> Wherefore I dare not, I, put forth my hand
> To hold the Ark, although it seem to shake
> Through th' old sinnes and new doctrines of our land.
> Onely, since God doth often vessels make
> Of lowly matter for high uses meet,
>> I throw me at his feet.
>
> There will I lie, untill my Maker seek
> For some mean stuffe whereon to show his skill:
> Then is my time. . .

However this delay in a man already convinced is not mere perversity. It reflects an antinomy that remains whether Herbert acts or not, namely, that what is impossible for man is possible with God and, *vice versa*, that what is possible for God is still impossible for man. So it should be no surprise that subsequently, when Herbert has submitted to ordination, we should find him complaining that in spite of all he is no priest.

> Holinesse on the head,
> Light and perfections on the breast,
> Harmonious bells below raising the dead
> To lead them unto life and rest:
> Thus are true Aarons drest.
>
> Profanenesse in my head,
> Defects and darkness in my breast,
> A noise of passions ringing me for dead
> Unto a place where is no rest:
> Poore priest thus am I drest.
>
> Onely another head
> I have, another heart and breast,
> Another musick, making live not dead,
> Without whom I could have no rest:
> In him I am well drest.

Christ is my onely head,
My alone onely heart and breast,
My onely musick, striking me ev'n dead;
That to the old man I may rest,
And be in him new drest.

So holy in my head,
Perfect and light in my deare breast,
My doctrine tun'd by Christ, (who is not dead,
But lives in me while I do rest)
Come people; Aaron's drest.

('Aaron')

Simply as verse this is a remarkable poem, discriminatingly drawn and handling the finest of points with assurance. Great perturbation of spirit and great exaltation are contained within an elegant, economical structure. There is chastity in the lines and, at the same time, Herbert's playful irony, his poet's delight in the full savour of words.

The basic image is simple. Herbert meditates on Aaron as we read of him in Exodus 28, robed in the sacred tunic with golden bells and pomegranates along its border, with the words 'Holiness unto the Lord' on a golden plate upon the forehead and the jewelled breastplate containing the Urim and Thummim (Lights and Perfections) upon his breast; and he asks himself how he compares with that.

The irony of the poem stands in this comparison which Herbert handles with what seems to be perfect innocence and yet must know to be outrageously contentious. The word *priest* was one of the most hotly disputed terms of the Reformation, and Herbert's own ministry was carried out during a time of vigorous puritanism when many people were refusing to apply the term to a Christian minister. Nevertheless, at the one point in the poem where he uses the word, Herbert applies it, not to Aaron, which would be unexceptionable, but to himself.

Poore priest, thus am I drest.

To compound the irony and outrage further, Herbert handles the matter through the image of priestly vesture. In another poet that might be merely polemical. With Herbert the intention is plainly poetic.

The image needs to be taken with the argument it carries and with the very form and sound of the poem, all of which make up an extraordinary unity.

Herbert's metrical devices are often fascinating in themselves and the more fascinating in the way he makes them serve the total intention of his verse. Here, we notice, there are only two rhyme sounds and five rhyme words which appear in the same order in each of five verses: *head, breast, dead, rest* and *drest*. The poem is thus an exploration of the interrelated meanings of these five words though, of course, four are so obviously interrelated as to need no demonstration. Head and breast, mind and heart, engage quite naturally with the prospect of death and the hope of rest. But to explore these sombre ideas within a poem whose apparent theme is clothing and whose continual refrain is the word *drest* is a matter of much ingenuity.

Now ingenuity is always at work in Herbert's poetry. A man who can compare the attractiveness of God with a pulley and prayer with an artillery battle, is not likely to balk at comparing his own priesthood with Aaron's robes. The stone upon which all this is founded, though, which we must either stumble at or prepare with Herbert to build upon, is the claim that this imaginative ingeniousness can actually serve the needs of faith—is, indeed, a proper way of doing theology. Certainly it will be theology of a special type. There will be no scholastic distinctions, no arguments built up from critically achieved definitions. There will be few ideas that can be carried around from one job to the next like the tools of a technician. But there will be, as we see in Herbert that there is, a direct engagement with experience and a true confession of faith in Christ within its many complexities.

Herbert, then, is exploiting the resources of his own style of poetry—the far-fetched conceit, the play on words, the deliberate ambiguity—to serve a theological purpose that cannot otherwise be accomplished. Here the antinomies which inform that complex reality, the Christian ministry, can be stated, not as disjunctions, but as the union in one experience of diverse but necessary truths. According to this poem, Aaronic priesthood (which stands for all natural, religious priesthood) and Christian ministry have and yet have not something in common. The denial and the affirmation are equally important, hard as it has

17

been in the history of doctrine to hold them together.

Let us consider the affirmative aspect first. Herbert clearly had no qualms about using the word *priest* of himself, and in that he was supported by the considered usage of the Church of England. However, it is not merely a word that he uses but an idea or image of priesthood. He sees the Christian minister's calling to be shaped or patterned in a priestly way. The picture of Aaron standing robed before the people of God acts as a ruling conceit organising all the material of the poem, shaping the poet's exposition of his own experience of priesthood. With that image goes one unavoidable affirmation, that priesthood is a social institution, a form through which people are related to one another as well as to God. The priest's clothing stands for this public aspect of priestliness. The climax of the poem is not merely, 'Aaron's drest', but , 'Come people; Aaron's drest'. Controversy has so centred upon the sacrificial function of priesthood that its more general social aspect has tended to be overlooked. In every society that is held together by a common allegiance certain people are singled out for the sake of the rest, to act as a focus for that allegiance. And where the allegiance is in any way directed toward God we can properly call those singled out a priesthood. The priest's calling is to represent to mankind at large those things which are considered most vital to the life of man, those truths which are saving truths because they are sacred and sacred because they are saving.

Herbert offers a charming Christian interpretation of this in his understanding of the bells. According to Exodus, Aaron was to wear bells on the skirt of his robe in order that he might not die—that is, presumably, that he might not be struck down for infringing the taboo set upon drawing near to God. For Herbert, however, not to die is a promise of the Gospel: it means the deathlessness of Christ's resurrection communicated to the whole Church.

> Harmonious bells below, raising the dead
> To lead them unto life and rest:

It is these *dead*, raised to life and led to rest through the Gospel who are the priest's people.

This is a version, (highly coloured if you like) of the doctrine of the

18

Anglican Ordinal. As it says in the ordination prayer, the ministry is appointed for the salvation of mankind. Its task is to communicate to men that knowledge of God in Christ, that vital truth, that fellowship in holy things which will secure their eternal salvation. As the bishop says to those about to be ordained, as Herbert says to himself through this image, 'Have always therefore printed upon your remembrance how great a treasure is committed to your charge. For they are the sheep of Christ'.

Now it was this sense of responsibility to Christ on behalf of his people which Herbert experienced every day and which was illuminated for him by the image of the priesthood. Therefore he affirms it. This affirmation, nevertheless, is far from being a dry, technical or, indeed, straightforward matter. He is led by the Gospel to stand back from it— to criticise it even as he uses it, to deny it even as he affirms it. The picture of Aaron which he takes from Exodus and hands on to us (already strangely altered) is not a prescription, not a theological definition: it is a conceit, an analogy, a type. It begins from priesthood conceived in the most external, institutional terms, where literally the vestments make the priest and sounding bells deliver a man from death, but it breaks open to a wholly new dimension, where the garments of priesthood are an inner clothing and the sound of bells is the voice of Christ heard upon the lips of the one whom he has sent.

And that leads on to a deeper and more radical denial of the image, for if priesthood is not vestments and bells but holiness, light, perfection, harmony and the word of life, then who is worthy to be a priest? Understood in these terms priesthood is the impossible vocation. No man can receive it for no man can respond to it.

Here indeed Herbert is a true child of the Reformation with its sense of the radical emptiness of all human claims in relation to God. If it is God you are dealing with there is nowhere for you to begin, no ground on which you can stand or make a move. Or rather, since the Reformation is gospel as well as dogma, there is no ground but Christ—the ground which God has provided within himself. The centre of this poem is the point at which Herbert first names the name of Christ. The intercourse with God which is impossible to man on his own is wholly possible, natural and free for man in Christ. This theological affirmation is basic to the poem as it is to Herbert's life. The grace of Christ is the beginning, continuation and completion of everything. All doctrines are subordinate to this doctrine, all holy acts are performed by virtue of this promise, that we are made worthy, justified and renewed by the grace of God in Christ.

So Christ is the source, sustainer and fulfilment of our priesthood. And more—he is our priesthood. That is the answer, and a sufficient answer, to our unworthiness.

> Christ is my onely head,
> My alone onely heart and breast,
> My onely musick, striking me ev'n dead;
> That to the old man I may rest,
> And be in him new drest.

'THE FLOWER'

How fresh, O Lord, how sweet and clean
Are thy returns! ev'n as the flowers in spring;
    To which, besides their own demean,
The late-past frosts tributes of pleasure bring.
        Grief melts away
        Like snow in May,
    As if there were no such cold thing.

Who would have thought my shrivel'd heart
Could have recover'd greennesse? It was gone
    Quite underground; as flowers depart
To see their mother-root when they are blown;
        Where they together
        All the hard weather,
    Dead to the world, keep house unknown.

These are thy wonders, Lord of power,
Killing and quickning, bringing down to hell
    And up to heaven in an houre;
Making a chiming of a passing-bell.
        We say amisse,
        This or that is:
    Thy word is all, if we could spell.

O that I once past changing were,
Fast in thy Paradise where no flower can wither!
    Many a spring I shoot up fair,
Offring at heav'n, growing and groning thither:
        Nor doth my flower
        Want a spring-showre,
    My sinnes and I joining together.

But while I grow in a straight line,
Still upwards bent, as if heav'n were mine own.
Thy anger comes, and I decline:
What frost to that? what pole is not the zone,
Where all things burn,
When thou dost turn,
And the least frown of thine is shown?

And now in age I bud again,
After so many deaths I live and write;
I once more smell the dew and rain,
And relish versing: O my onely light,
It cannot be
That I am he
On whom thy tempests fell all night.

These are thy wonders, Lord of love,
To make us see we are but flowers that glide:
Which when we once can finde and prove,
Thou hast a garden for us where to bide.
Who would be more,
Swelling through store,
Forfeit their Paradise by their pride.

('The Flower')

We experience these alternatives ourselves, from winter to spring, death to life, confinement to release, hell to heaven. We experience them, but how do we react to them? Not perhaps, like Herbert, with poetry, but at least with that which Herbert expresses through his poetry—with prayer. Can we learn from this poem how a man of Herbert's faith would pray?

We have seen already that he would not ignore the circumstances or the emotions of the moment when he came to pray. He prays as he is and as he feels. He cries to God out of the depths and he praises him upon the heights. He encounters God in the mood of the moment, just as he had prayed in the well-known hymn, to see him in all things.

Nevertheless, God's manner of being in all things, or (if we prefer) our manner of perceiving him there, are problematical. How do we share with God the things that happen to us when God's presence in them is not transparently clear to us and some seem actively detrimental to us? Somewhere between seeing them as a direct consequence of his will and behaving as though they have nothing to do with him, we have to seek a middle way in which things and events can be themselves and yet be the focus of our fellowship with him. The ancient Hebrews attributed everything to God directly; for them there were no intermediate causes. In our time we are more disposed to see God as wholly removed from the processes of the world. Our prayer aspires to an angelic quality, a pure intention beyond every event that happens and everything it happens to. If such prayer makes a difference, it is only because we ourselves, as believers, are different. God enters our world only through our faith.

There is, however, another way still, neither totally objective nor totally subjective—the way of Christ's Incarnation. In Christ God has himself shared the human condition and that establishes both the possibility and the pattern of our sharing it with God.

Herbert's arrangement of his poems was deliberate, so it is no accident that this poem, 'The Flower', with its theme of renewal and resurrection is preceded immediately by a poem called 'The Crosse'. But it is also no accident that the second poem is not actually called 'The Resurrection'. There is a complexity to it that makes it something more than an Easter morning hymn and which reflects Herbert's sense that the way we correlate our own experience with God's experience in Christ also has its own complexity.

'The Crosse' is one of the poems of Herbert's priesthood, a period which, in the light of all that had passed, we might expect to have been pure joy. Clearly it was not so. Perhaps the progress of the disease that finally killed him, perhaps simply a depressive mood with whatever physical concomitants, seizing him for no apparent reason, deprived him of the stisfaction that ordination might have brought.

> And then when after much delay,
> Much wrastling, many a combate, this deare end,
> So much desir'd, is giv'n, to take away
> My power to serve thee; to unbend

> All my abilities, my designes confound,
> And lay my threatnings bleeding on the ground.
>
> One ague dwelleth in my bones,
> Another in my soul (the memorie
> What I would do for thee, if once my grones
> Could be allow'd for harmonie):
> I am in all a weak disabled thing,
> Save in the sight thereof, where strength doth sting.

('The Crosse')

This poem is conceived dramatically, the poet shifting his thoughts with every new perspective on his trouble, but in the closing verse he comes to the only resting place possible for a Christian in his suffering. He is already approaching that point when he calls upon God as 'deare Father', even though his complaints continue for a moment. It is the Englishman's way of saying 'Abba'.

> Ah my deare Father, ease my smart!
> These contrarieties crush me: these crosse actions
> Do winde a rope about, and cut my heart:
> And yet since these thy contradictions
> Are properly a crosse felt by thy Sonne,
> With but foure words, my words, *Thy will be done*.

('The Crosse')

Whatever else is denied him the Christian may have fellowship with Christ in Gethsemane, and before the cross. Not that these words, 'Thy will be done', are to be taken as words of resignation—an admission that God will have his way whatever we may do—but just as for Jesus they were a confession that he would bear this contradiction if obedience to his mission required it, so for Herbert they are an acknowledgement that in choosing the priesthood he was choosing this, even if he did not forsee it at the time.

So when, in the very next poem, we find Herbert saying that his shrivelled heart has 'recover'd greennesse' that suggests two things. The first is that the true affliction was indeed the 'ague in the soul', the inner contradiction, the emotional contraction, so that now an emotional change has brought about its healing. Depression has been succeeded by elation, contraction by expansion. Then secondly, it suggests that if the condition of contraction was an experience of the cross, this is now an experience of the resurrection. Yet in the very moment when Herbert himself might say that in 'The Flower'—is indeed saying it—his thoughts take another turn and he begins to say something quite different.

> These are thy wonders, Lord of power,
> Killing and quickning, bringing down to hell
> And up to heaven in an houre;
> Making a chiming of a passing-bell.
> We say amisse,
> This or that is:
> Thy word is all, if we could spell.
>
> O that I once past changing were . . . !

It is not the sense of exaltation, not the condition to which change has brought him, that finally secures his attention. Rather he comes to dwell upon the condition of change itself, for that remains and will remain his fundamental condition until a better resurrection than this takes place. The momentary hyperbole, by which he declared himself carried up to heaven, has been recognised for the emptiness it is.

The significance of this sudden shift in Herbert's exposition of the matter has far-reaching consequences and forces us to think further about his meaning in 'The Crosse'. Momentarily a mood of expansiveness, release, happiness, has been compared with resurrection. That agrees well, of course, with the common practice of speaking of our 'cross' whenever we experience pain, humiliation or confinement, but that is not Herbert's practice. What Herbert says in his poem is only superficially the same thing; his judgement was too fine to allow him to conclude a poem or address himself to God with a sentiment so misleading or banal. He did not in fact say that his suffering was his 'cross': what he actually wrote is significantly different.

> And yet since these thy contradictions
> Are properly a crosse felt by thy Sonne . . .
>
> ('The Crosse')

25

Not *by me* but *by thy Sonne*, for it is Christ who suffers the Christian's pain redemptively. Herbert does not simply assume, as an interpretation given him with his sufferings, that he is crucified with Christ. He sees that he must appropriate the cross, and fellowship with Christ in the cross, by a deliberate act of faith and self-consecration. He must make Christ's words his own. He becomes a fellow-sufferer with Christ not by complaint nor by silence, but by that trust which is first of all Christ's and only then ours. For it is not simply in suffering contradiction but in suffering it for his sake that we are crucified with Christ; not in being killed but in self-surrender, whether to life or death; not through the emotions or sensations but through faith.

According to a certain Old Testament way of looking at things, all forms of prosperity, health, success and riches are signs of God's favour. It is easy to assume that while the New Testament dismisses this at the material level it confirms it in a more inward 'spiritual' way. Not outward but inward prosperity is then indeed a sign of God's favour, and the more valuable now that the full extent of his favour has been revealed. What such inward prosperity is taken to be differs from person to person, group to group. It may be peace of mind, emotional delight or mystical expansion. If this is how we see it, though, our spirituality will become simply an organised pattern of covetousness directed towards such things. That they are attractive states is obviously true. That they serve to confirm the promise of the Gospel is quite another matter.

So in the moment when Herbert starts to take pleasure before God in just such an attractive state, he hesitates and moves into another theme.

> We say amisse,
> This or that is:
> Thy word is all, if we could spell.

From his changing, changed condition Herbert has caught a glimpse of God's eternity, and having done so realises that he must interpret his newly recovered happiness with modesty. It is not this or that— this contraction or that expansion— which is the true reality and the Christian's true security, but the Word of God. The fairest gifts, the most free delights, breaking in upon our depressed condition, relieve our misery but also serve to remind us of the transitory state which is ours and beyond which our true rest lies. Thankful wonder then is converted to longing love. God who has been seen as the agent of change is now seen above and beyond it, and in that aspect is even more to be praised than before. In the last verse of the poem Herbert repeats his thanksgiving but with a significant alteration. He had called God 'Lord of power'. Now he says,

> These are thy wonders, Lord of love,
> To make us see we are but flowers that glide:
> Which when we once can finde and prove,
> Thou hast a garden for us where to bide.

The poet and priest who has taught so many of us to see God 'in all things' has a further lesson for us here: to see God beyond all things in the constancy of his promise. So also he calls us from a prayer enclosed in the present moment to one which begins in the present moment but longs hopefully for eternity. Certainly the experience of freedom and joy can be seen as a momentary confirmation of that hope, but confirmation is not fulfilment—fulfilment lies ahead. The truth grasped in the last line of 'The Crosse' is nowhere repented of. The gift we are given now to possess without qualification is to share Christ's agony in our own experience. We cannot with equal truth claim that we share in his Resurrection, for that would be to say that we had left the agony behind and were past change. Herbert, surprisingly perhaps (but the negative truth is needed to enforce what he has been saying positively), ends 'The Flower' with severe words against those who claim, as it were, that for them the resurrection has already taken place. We know the power of Christ's Resurrection now within the fellowship of his sufferings.

FAIRACRES PUBLICATIONS
Complete List

All titles listed above are obtainable—postage extra—from:
SLG PRESS Convent of the Incarnation Fairacres Oxford OX4 1TB

Price list April 1980